Before They Were Famous

# Walt Disney

Written by Stephen Krensky
Illustrated by Bobbie Houser

A Crabtree Crown Book

# School-to-Home Support for Caregivers and Teachers

This book is designed to teach and appeal to a student on core subject areas. The student will build upon what they already know about the subject and engage in topics that they do not know but want to learn more about. Here are a few guiding questions to help the reader on his or her comprehension skills. Possible answers appear here in red.

## Before Reading:

*What do I know about this topic?*

- *I know that Walt Disney was one of the pioneer artists in animation.*
- *I know that Walt's first successful animated character was Micky Mouse.*

*What do I want to learn about this topic?*

- *I want to learn more about the techniques that were used to make the cartoon characters move.*
- *I want to learn more about the relationship between Walt Disney and his brother Roy.*

## During Reading:

*I'm curious to know...*

- *I'm curious to know why Walt Disney went to high school for only one year.*
- *I'm curious to know why Walt wanted to become an ambulance driver in France during World War I.*

*How is this like something I already know?*

- *I know that not everyone has to go to school to become great at something.*
- *I know that it took Walt Disney a long time to become the creative genius he eventually became.*

## After Reading:

*What was the author trying to teach me?*

- *I think the author was trying to teach me that you must have perseverance and never quit when you have a dream for yourself to achieve great things.*
- *I think the author was trying to teach me that learning from early failures can help you achieve great things in life.*

*How did the photographs and captions help me understand more?*

- *I didn't know that Walt Disney used a pushcart to deliver newspapers in the mornings and evenings when he was a young boy.*
- *I didn't know that Walt drew his very successful cartoon character Micky Mouse while riding on a train after a disappointing job experience in New York City.*

# Table of Contents

# Picturing the Present

Young Walt Disney was pretty pleased with himself. Here he was, a new student at his Chicago high school. He had started out a complete unknown. And yet, after only a month, he was already the cartoonist for the school magazine.

Walter Elias Disney

McKinley High School

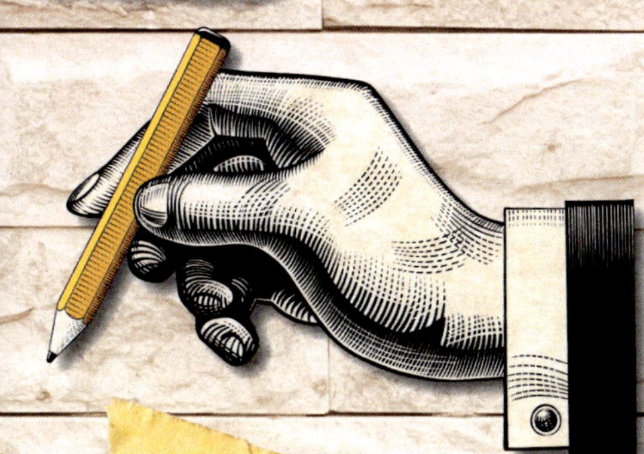

President William McKinley

## Fun Facts

Walt went to William McKinley High School, named after the American president who had been assassinated in 1901.

Walt had liked to draw for as long as he could remember. Even in class, he spent hours **doodling** characters in slightly different positions on the pages of his textbooks. Later, he would show his classmates what he had done. If he **riffled** the pages just right, the blur of pictures made it look like the characters were moving.

## Fun Facts

One of Disney's favorite actors, Charlie Chaplin, first introduced his most famous character, "The Tramp," in a film in 1914.

# Growing Up Fast

When Walt wasn't drawing, he liked to be in the middle of things. As he later recalled, "I'd do anything to attract attention."

### Fun Facts

Some of the people who had actually heard Lincoln himself recite the *Gettysburg Address* were still alive when Walt was imitating him.

One time in fifth grade, Walt made a cardboard stovepipe hat, drew a fake wart on his cheek, and came to school dressed as Abraham Lincoln. Standing in front of his class, he went on to **recite** the president's famous *Gettysburg Address*.

But Walt's life was not always fun. The Disneys had just enough money to get by. To help out, Walt and his older brother Roy walked long newspaper routes to deliver the morning and afternoon Kansas City newspapers.

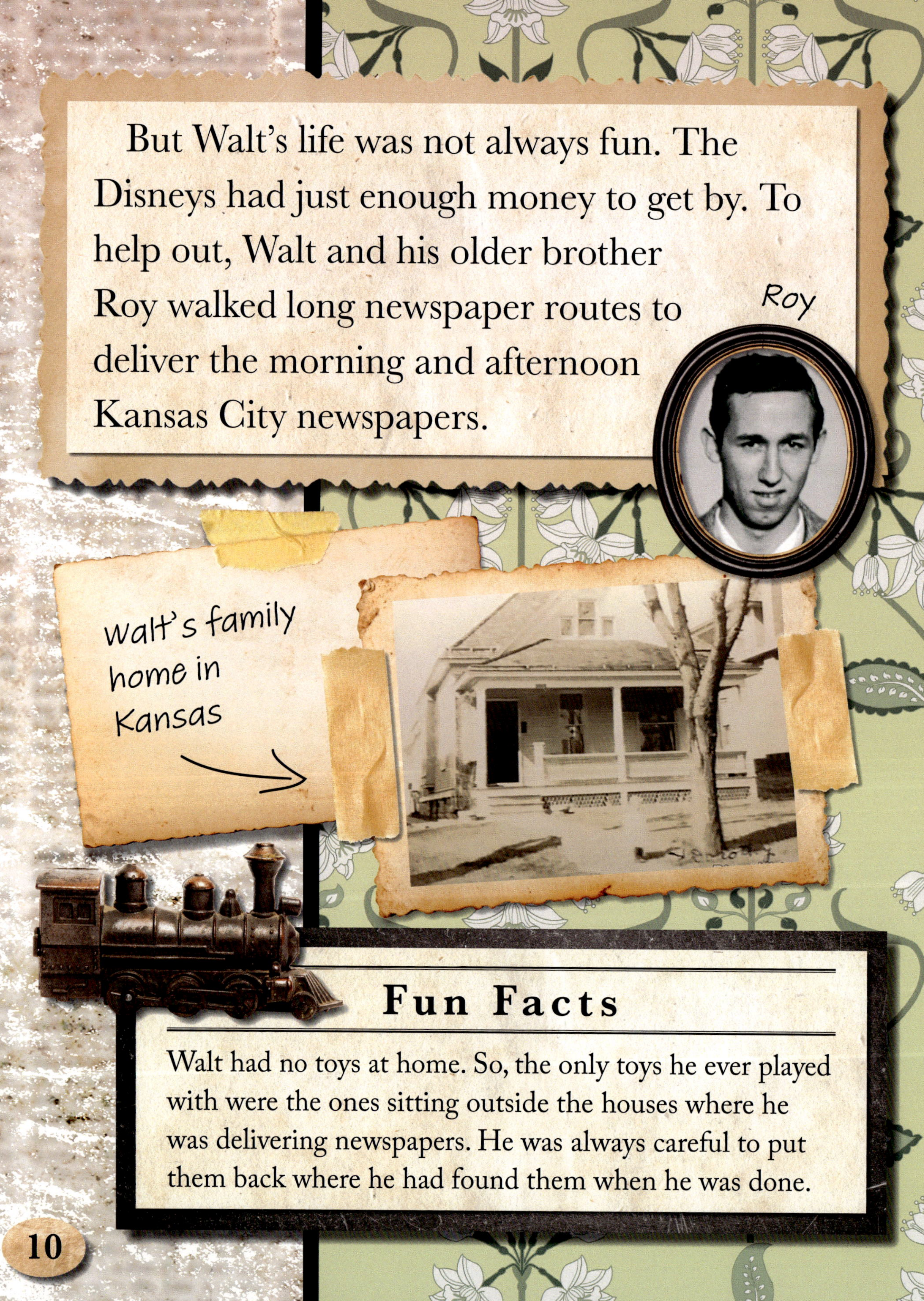


## Fun Facts

Walt had no toys at home. So, the only toys he ever played with were the ones sitting outside the houses where he was delivering newspapers. He was always careful to put them back where he had found them when he was done.

For six years they rose before dawn to complete the morning route before school. Then they repeated the route late in the afternoon. Unfortunately, they did not own a horse and wagon to help with the job and had to deliver the newspapers with pushcarts.

As much as Walt liked being the cartoonist for the school newspaper, he spent only one year in high school before moving on. In 1917, the United States had entered World War I. Walt wanted to **enlist**. But at 16, he was too young to serve in the army.

Walt Disney enlisted in the Red Cross Ambulance Corps.

However, with his mother's signed permission, he was able to become an ambulance driver for the Red Cross in France. He spent one week learning to drive ambulances and trucks, a second week learning how to repair them, and then two more weeks doing military drills.

After that, he was ready to go.

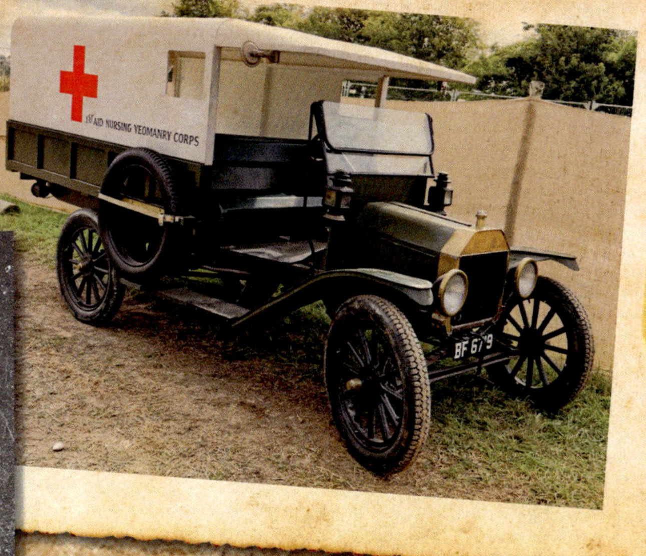

## Fun Facts

The first gasoline-powered ambulance was produced in 1905.

# A Trip Abroad

Walt landed in France at the beginning of December 1918, just a few days before his 17th birthday. The war had ended, but the Red Cross still needed drivers to help care for wounded soldiers.

Walt's driving duties kept him busy. But in his spare time, he returned to drawing. He decorated the **canteen** menu with cartoons and drew exaggerated **caricatures** of soldiers that they shared with their families back home.

Somewhere in France
April 10th 1919

Dear School Chums:

Well, how is every thing around McKinley high School? Fine. I just remembered that I owed a letter to my old school paper, so here it is. Well, I am feeling fine to-day and hope every one back home is the same. I am fine also having a time and working hard. I am stationed in Neufchatau not far from Chaumont the headquarters of Gen. Pershing.

France is an interesting place but just the same I want to — to —.

Well so-long or Aureovoir for this time Hope-ing to see all of you soon. I remain as ever your old artist

APO 731. Neufchatau France

Walt also discovered, he remembered later, “that the inside and the outside of an ambulance was as good a place to draw as any.”

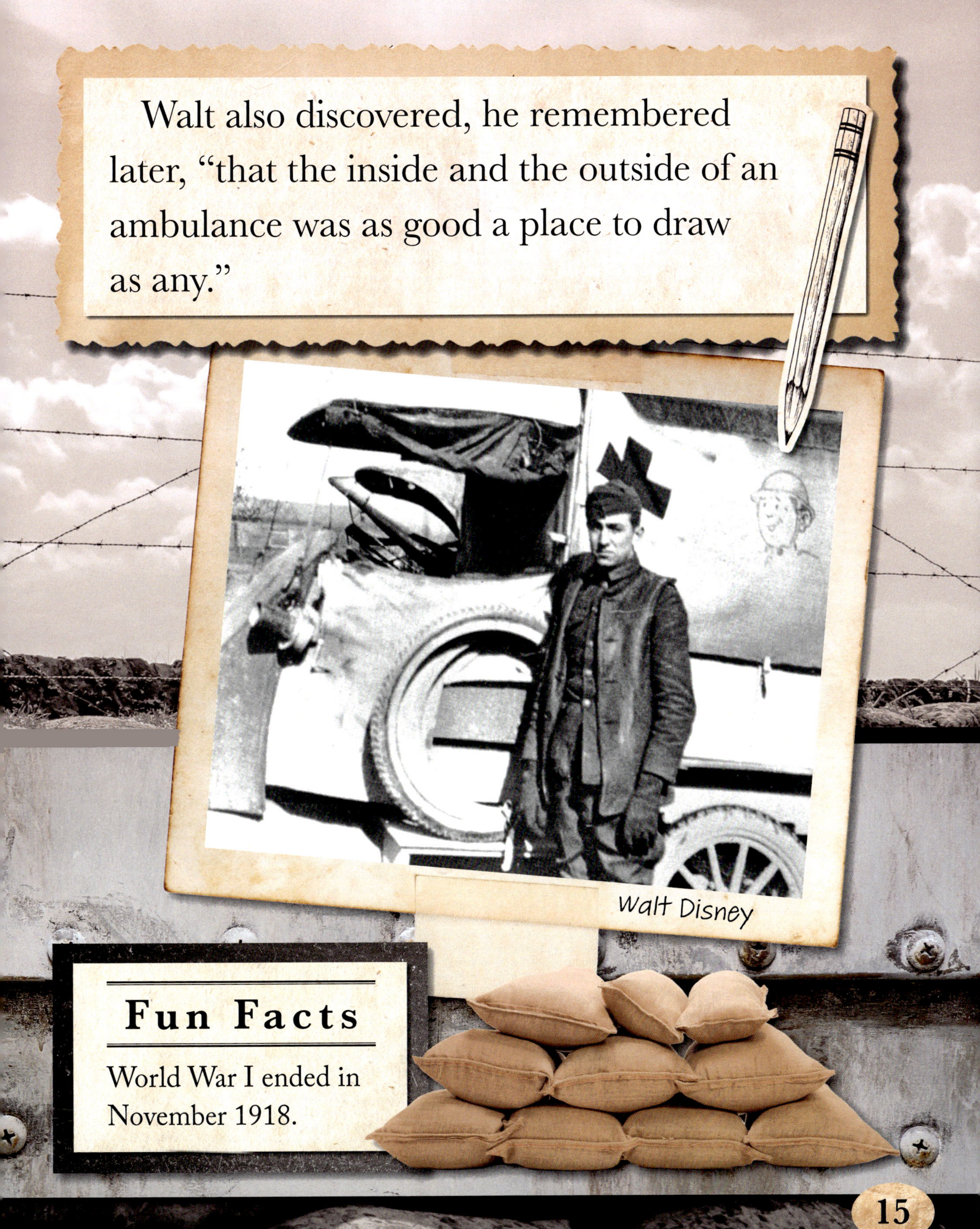

Walt Disney

**Fun Facts**

World War I ended in November 1918.

When Walt returned home near the end of 1919, he found work as a **commercial** artist. None of his early jobs lasted very long. But in the next year, he developed a new passion — **animation**. The art and craft "of making things move on film is what got me," he later explained.

## Fun Facts

In 1919, the cartoon character *Felix the Cat* became the first cartoon to be **merchandised.**

Walt also loved the fact that animation was still a new field. It gave him the chance of becoming better at it than anyone else.

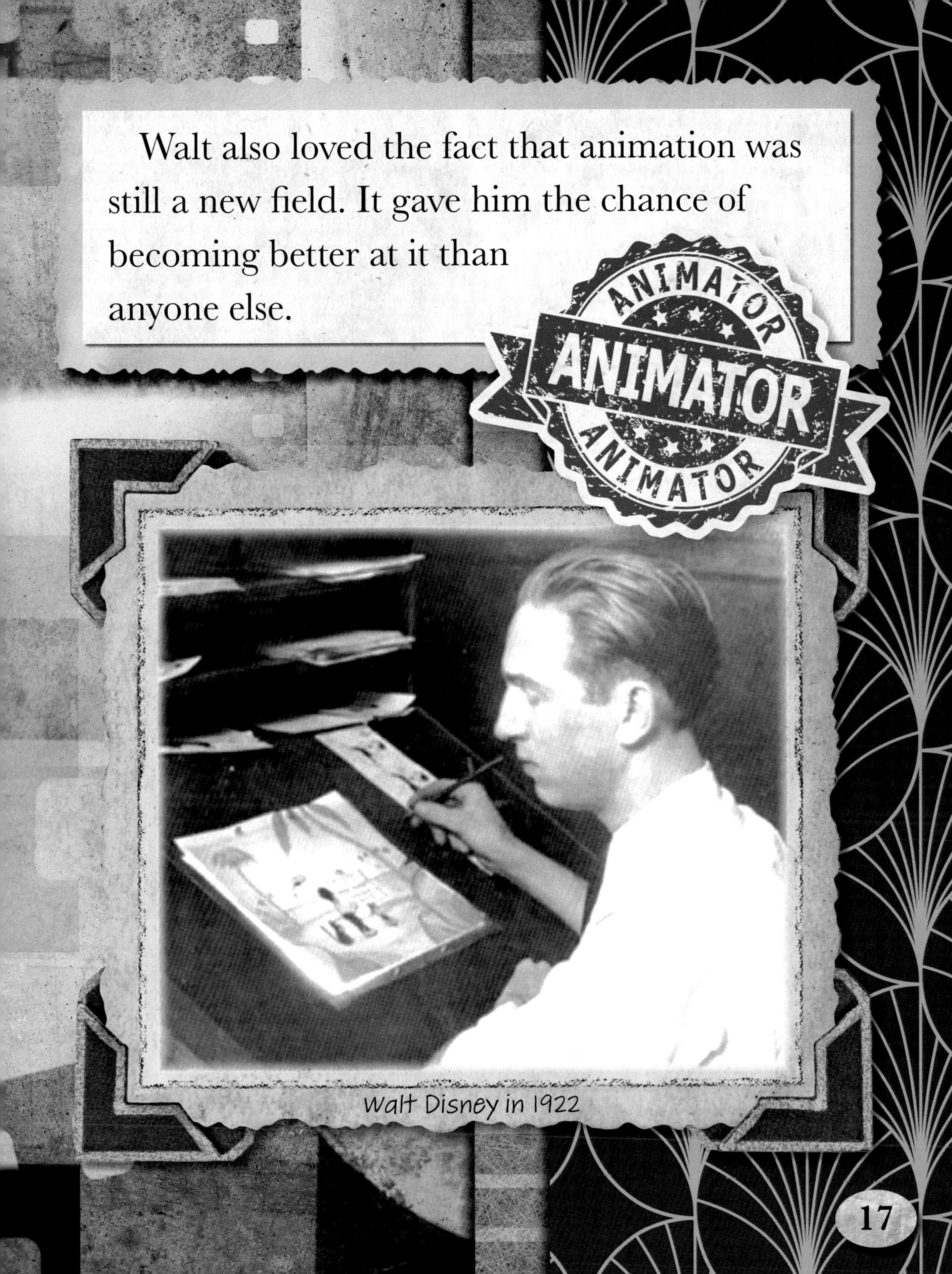


Walt Disney in 1922

# Artful Development

Before long, Walt was working with a new partner, a fellow artist with the distinctive name of Ub Iwerks. Together they created short, animated films called Laugh-O-grams that were shown all over the country.

Ub Iwerks

Child Actress Virginia Davis starred in *Alice's Wonderland*.

**Fun Facts**

One of Disney's early creative ideas was to make a film in which a young live-action actress would mix with animated characters. He called it *Alice's Wonderland*.

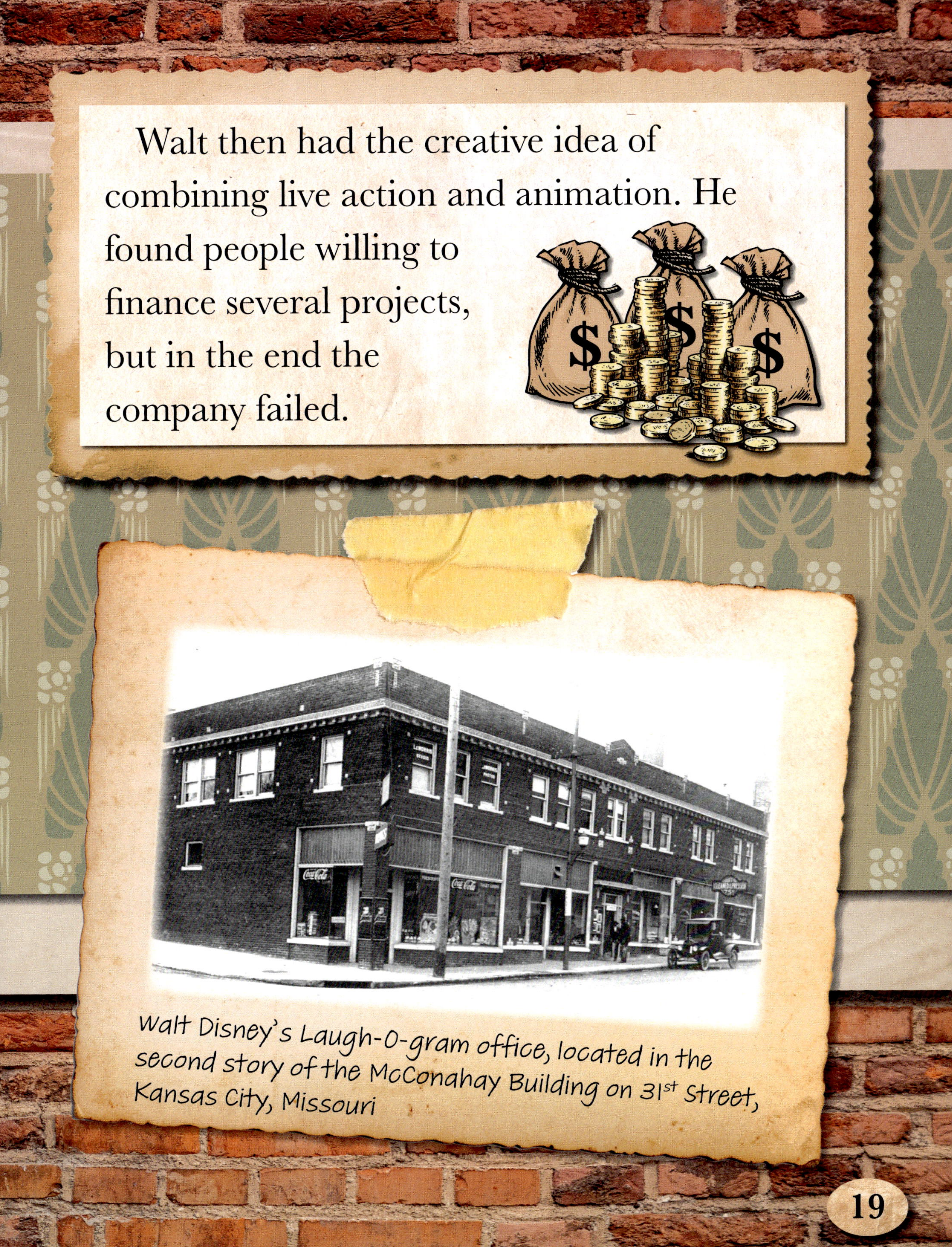

Walt then had the creative idea of combining live action and animation. He found people willing to finance several projects, but in the end the company failed.

Walt Disney's Laugh-O-gram office, located in the second story of the McConahay Building on 31st Street, Kansas City, Missouri

Walt took a deep breath and decided to make a really fresh start in a completely new place. In the summer of 1923, with only a few dollars in his pocket, he headed for Los Angeles. A lot of new films were being made in an area called Hollywood. Besides, his brother Roy was living there, too.

D. W. Griffith, American director of the film *In Old California*

## Fun Facts

The first film shot in Hollywood, *In Old California*, was made in 1910.

Greetings from
HOLLYWOOD
CALIFORNIA
Roy
Walt
BROTHERS

# Westward Bound

MADE IN LOS ANGELES MADE IN

Walt was ready to start a new company, but he knew better than to think he could do it alone. Ub Iwerks soon came west to join him, but Walt also convinced Roy to be his partner. They called the company *The Disney Brothers Cartoon Studio.* Before long they decided a different name would be better. And what did Walt pick? Well, he thought the name *Walt Disney Studio* had a nice ring to it.

Walt Disney Studios 1926-1940

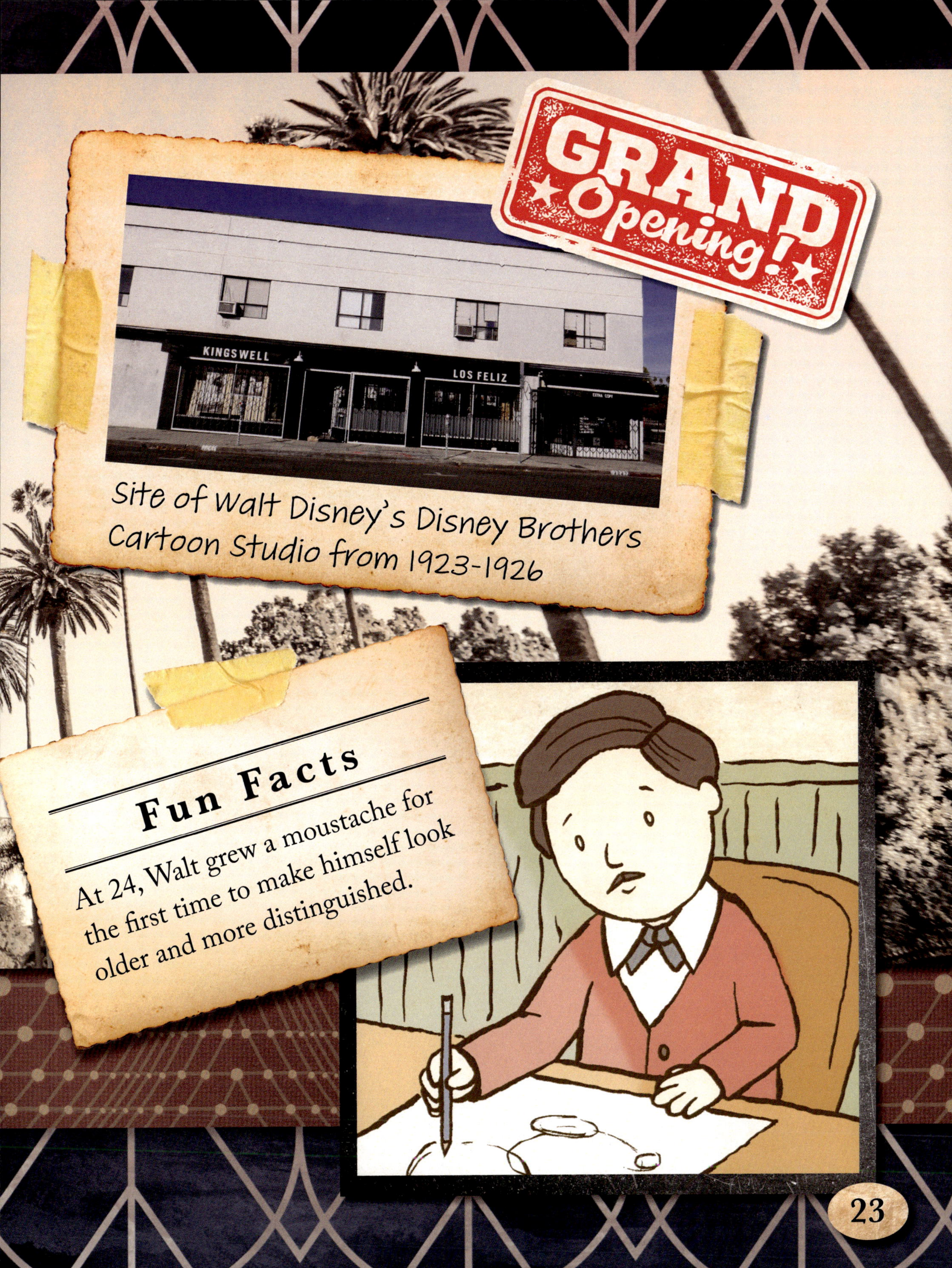


Site of Walt Disney's Disney Brothers Cartoon Studio from 1923-1926

## Fun Facts

At 24, Walt grew a moustache for the first time to make himself look older and more distinguished.

Their first major project was a series about a real girl named Alice. She was the star of *Alice's Comedies*, in which she and an animated cat named Julius had a series of funny adventures.

Julius

## Fun Facts

The first film with sound as well as pictures, *The Jazz Singer*, came out in 1927.

One of the studio's first employees, who was hired to do inking was a young woman named Lillian Bounds. As Walt and Lillian got to know each other better, they became a couple, then a serious couple, and finally, a married couple.

Walt and Lillian

Later, Walt's film **distributor** asked him to create a new character, a rabbit that would star in its own series.

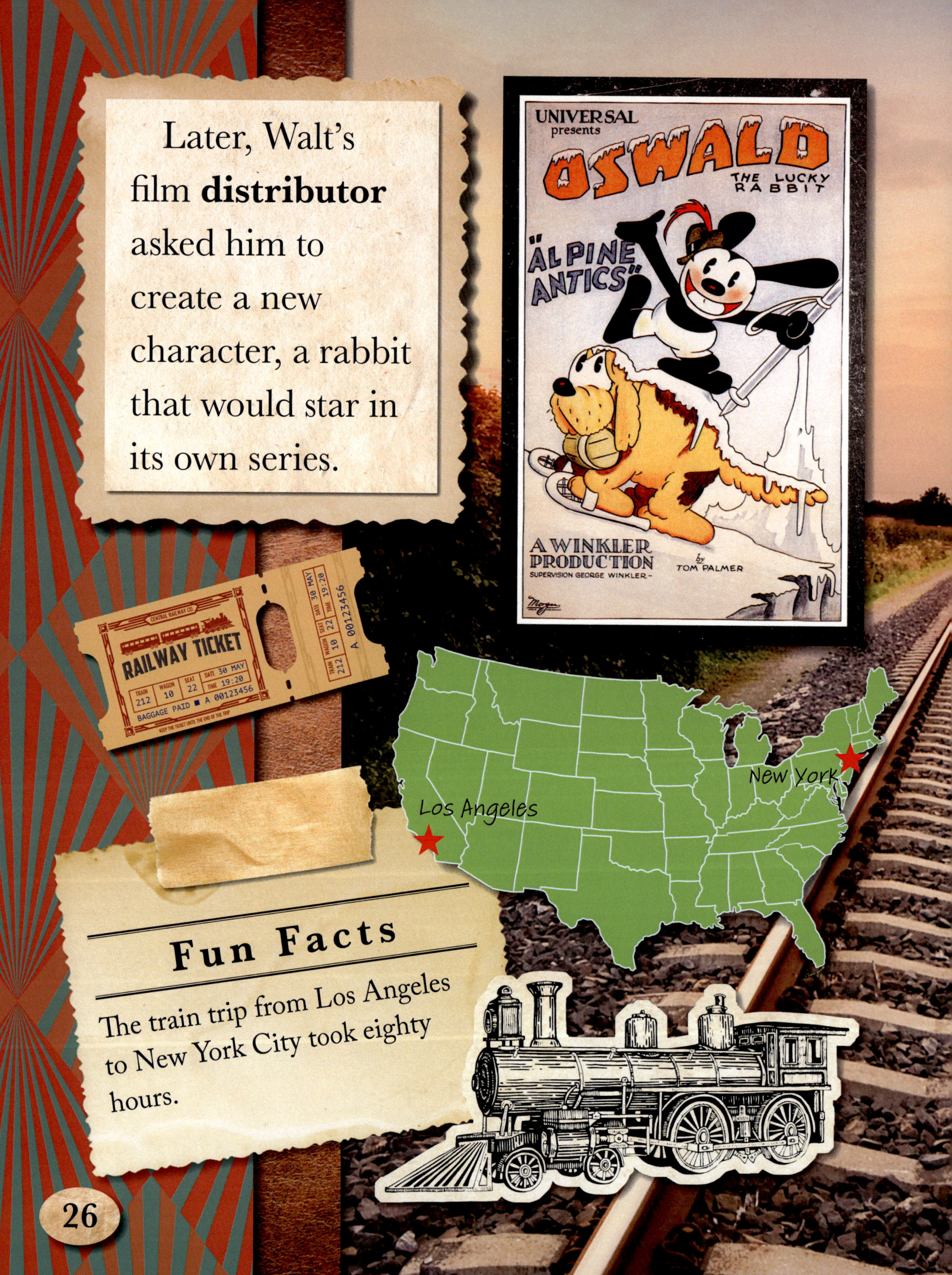


## Fun Facts

The train trip from Los Angeles to New York City took eighty hours.

It took a while for Oswald the Lucky Rabbit to be fully developed. Once the character was completed Walt and Lillian went to New York City to work out what Walt expected to be a new long-term contract. Instead, he found himself squeezed out of the series with no legal ownership of Oswald. If Oswald became a hit, the distributor would benefit, not Walt.

On the long trip back to Los Angeles, Walt began drawing a new animal character, a mouse named Mortimer. And going to New York had taught him a valuable lesson. From now on, Walt would make sure that any characters he created would belong to his company.

When he showed Mortimer to Lillian, she liked the character well enough. But the name wasn't quite right. She had a better one in mind.

Walt wasn't sure he liked her name at first. After a little more thought, he finally agreed with her. By the time they got back home, the character's new name was settled.

He was called Mickey Mouse.

## Fun Facts

Mickey Mouse's first appearance was in a 1928 cartoon called *Steamboat Willie.*

*Walter Elias Disney was born on December 5, 1901, in Chicago, Illinois. His fondest memories of growing up were spent on the farm near Marceline, Missouri, where his family lived from 1906 to 1911. The earliest big success of the Walt Disney Studio, founded with his brother Roy in 1927, was the introduction of Mickey Mouse in 1928. The first full-length Disney animated movie,* Snow White and the Seven Dwarfs, *became a milestone in the history of animation in 1937. Other successful Disney movies followed, as well as the opening of the theme parks Disneyland in 1954 and Disney World in 1971. Walt Disney himself died in 1966 at the age of 65.*

# GLOSSARY

**animation**
A group of slightly different drawings that create the illusion of movement when shown quickly in the right order

**canteen**
An informal restaurant often used by military services, camps, or companies to provide meals for those nearby

**caricatures**
Drawings in which facial features such as the nose and ears are exaggerated to make the drawings funny

**commercial**
To pay for work done

**distributor**
A person whose job is to help a product reach its intended customers

**doodling**
Casual drawings or sketches, often with very little detail

**enlist**
To join or sign up for

**merchandised**
Sold as a product

**recite**
To say aloud a poem or speech from memory

**riffled**
Flipped quickly through pages

# INDEX



# COMPREHENSION QUESTIONS

In what city did Walt start high school?

Where did Walt work with the Red Cross?

What was the first name of the company that Walt founded with his brother Roy?

## ABOUT THE AUTHOR

Stephen Krensky is the award-winning author of more than 150 fiction and nonfiction books for children. He and his wife Joan live in Lexington, Massachusetts, and he happily spends as much time as possible with his grown children and not-so-grown grandchildren.

Written by: Stephen Krensky
Illustrations by: Bobbie Houser
Designed by: Bobbie Houser
Series Development: James Earley
Proofreader: Kathy Middleton
Educational Consultant: Marie Lemke M.Ed.

Photographs:
t = Top, c = Center, b = Bottom, l = Left, r = Right

Alamy: WALT DISNEY/Ronald Grant Archive: cover tl, p. 29 t; Chicago History Museum: p. 5 tl; JT Vintage: p. 7 tl; Album: p. 7 br, 24 br; History and Art Collection: p. 10 tr; ARCHIVIO GBB: p. 15 c; Moviestore Collection: p. 16 bl; Photo12/Collection 7e Art: p. 18 tr; Collection Christophel: p. 18 bl; Pictorial Press: p. 20 bl; Masheter Movie Archive: p. 22 b, 25 c; Barry King: p. 23 tl; The Picture Art Collection: p. 24 tr; Everett Collection: p. 26 tr; ancestralfindings.com: p. 4 l; Disney: p. 17 c, 21 c; disneyhistory101.com: p. 10 c; Getty: cover bl, p. 24 cl, 28, 29 br; Library of Congress: p. 5 bl; mickeynews.com: p. 12 br, 14; pendergastkc.org: p. 19 b; Shutterstock: Iaroslav Neliubov: cover br, p. 24 cr; Naumov S: p. 4 r; JosepPerianes: p. 5 tr; Maisei Raman: p. 5 cr; Nikiparonak: p. 6 tr, 15 tr; xactive: p. 7 tc; trekandshoot: p. 7 tr; Elena Pimonova: p. 7 bl; Alex_Bond: p. 8 t; Everett Collection: p. 8 b, 12 tl; glenda: p. 9 l; History and Art Collection: p. 10 bl; magicoven: p. 11 r; Aitor Serra Martin: p. 12 bl; ducu59us: p. 13 tr; Elena_Medvedeva: p. 13 l; Andrew Harker: p. 13 br; Ljupco Smokovski: p. 15 br; losw: p. 16 tr; designtools: p. 17 tr; Uncle Leo: p. 19 tr; Macrovector: p. 20 tr; Callahan: p. 21 tl; Nata_Alhontess: p. 21 tr; marekuliasz: p. 21 b; iQoncept: p. 22 tr; squarelogo: p. 23 tr; doomu: p. 25 tr; Julia Henze: p. 25 bl; Vector Tradition: p. 26 cl; Tanarch: p. 26 cr; Vorobiov Oleksii 8: p. 26 br; FrankHH: p. 27 c

**Crabtree Publishing**

**crabtreebooks.com 800-387-7650**



**Printed in Canada/012024/CP20231127**

**Published in Canada Crabtree Publishing**
616 Welland Ave.
St. Catharines, Ontario
L2M 5V6

**Published in the United States Crabtree Publishing**
347 Fifth Ave
Suite 1402-145
New York, NY 10016

**Library and Archives Canada Cataloguing in Publication**
Available at Library and Archives Canada

**Library of Congress Cataloging-in-Publication Data**
Available at the Library of Congress

Hardcover: 978-1-0398-3887-1
Paperback: 978-1-0398-3972-4
Ebook (pdf): 978-1-0398-4047-8
Epub: 978-1-0398-4119-2